THERE FOR THOS

THERE FOR THOSE IN PERIL

The Story of Minehead's RNLI Lifeboat Station.

Chris Rundle

THERE FOR THOSE IN PERIL

Copyright © 2024 Chris Rundle

All rights reserved.

ISBN:9798876929716

THERE FOR THOSE IN PERIL

Dedicated to all those who have served the RNLI at its Minehead station.

ACKNOWLEDGMENTS

Grateful thanks to Nick Leach, Phil Sanderson and Richard Newton for providing many of the images in this book. Thank you, also, to Tony White for his meticulous editing

THERE FOR THOSE IN PERIL

CONTENTS

1	STORMY BEGINNINGS	Pg 4
2	MEETING THE CHALLENGES	Pg 8
3	LIFEBOATS FOR THE NEW AGE	Pg 21
4	ON SERVICE	Pg 25
5	BIGGER AND FASTER	Pg 52
6	GOING OUT WITH A BANG	Pg 59
7	LADIES WHO LAUNCH	Pg 74
8	FIT FOR THE FUTURE	Pg 96
9	FIT FOR PURPOSE	Pg 103
10	THE LIFEBOAT FAMILY	Pg 116

THERE FOR THOSE IN PERIL

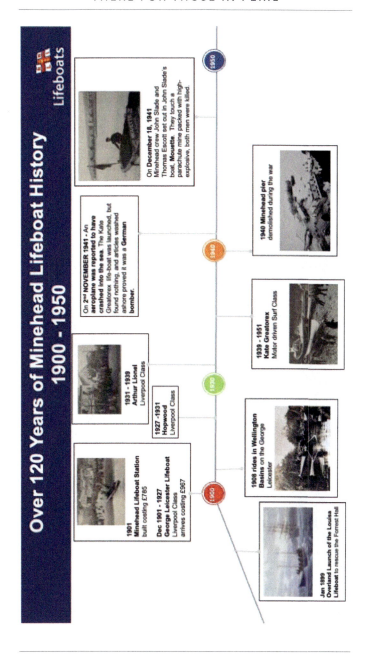

THERE FOR THOSE IN PERIL

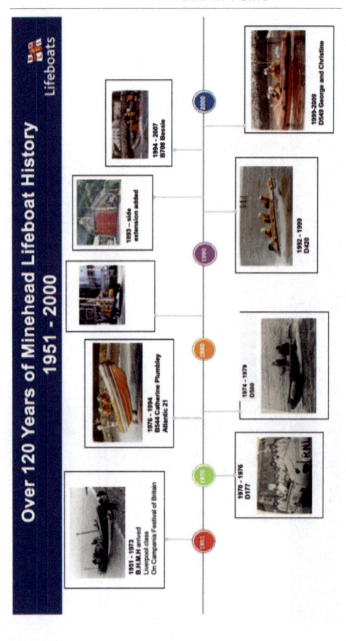

2

THERE FOR THOSE IN PERIL

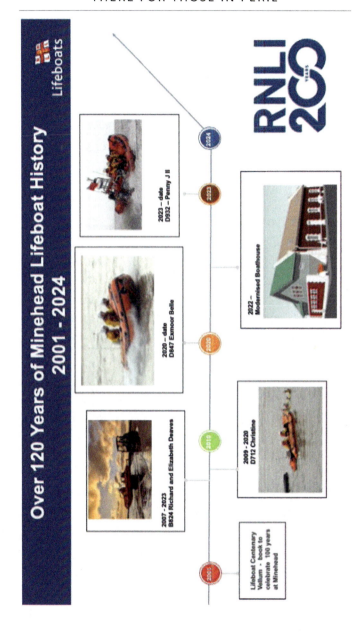

3

THERE FOR THOSE IN PERIL

1 STORMY BEGINNINGS

The story of Minehead lifeboat station really starts 18 miles westward in the tiny North Devon village of Lynmouth. Today it's a buzzing holiday resort but in the 19th century was just a remote, cliff-foot fishing community standing at the confluence of two rivers and more easily accessible by sea than by land.

It's January 12 1899 and a violent gale is whipping up huge waves in the Bristol Channel but just before eight in the evening Lynmouth lifeboat station receives a telegram: a schooner is in danger of being driven ashore in Porlock Bay - can the lifeboat launch?

THERE FOR THOSE IN PERIL

Coxswain Jack Crocombe needs only one sight of the sea state to know it's out of the question: if the boat - the Louisa - weren't engulfed while still on its carriage it risked capsizing trying to negotiate the huge breakers now crashing onto the pebble beach.

There is, Jack concludes, only one thing for it: hitch up a team of horses and tow the boat 13 miles to launch from the relative shelter of Porlock Weir.

No mean undertaking: the rough, unmetalled way to Porlock lay across the top of the Exmoor cliffs, the highest in England, soaring to more than 430 metres. At the start of the journey Countisbury Hill offered a mile-long, one in four gradient while at the other end was Porlock Hill with an equally steep but more tortuous descent.

But 18 lives were at stake aboard the 1,900 ton Forrest Hall, on passage from Bristol to Liverpool, and there was no time to hesitate.

The Overland Launch is still cited as one of the most epic in the entire, 200-year history of the RNLI and remains a moving testimonial to the determination of all its lifeboat crews.

Along the way to Porlock roadside walls had to be demolished to allow the boat to pass and at one narrow point it had to be slid off its carriage and dragged across fields on wooden skids. Part of a house had to be knocked down to negotiate the tight turn at the bottom of Porlock Hill.

But at 6.30 am the Lynmouth crew finally reached the sea and launched into the storm, standing by the Forrest Hall off Hurlestone Point until tugs arrived to take her in tow to Barry, on the South Wales coast. Even then the Lynmouth heroes weren't done: they set to the oars and escorted the battered schooner all the way to Wales. After a few hours' rest they were towed part way back across the channel then rowed home, arriving at 11.30am on January 14.

Aside from showcasing the bravery of RNLI volunteers the incident also revealed that there was a very large gap in lifeboat cover along the southern Bristol Channel coast: the nearest station east of Lynmouth was at Watchet where, equally, the foul weather had prevented a launch.

So Minehead was chosen as the site for an intermediate station. Land near the harbour was provided by its owner, the Luttrell family, and at a cost of £785 the lifeboat station was built and opened in 1901 with its first boat, the George Leicester, a non-self-righting Liverpool class, arriving on service in December that year.

2 MEETING THE CHALLENGES

On a chart, Minehead appeared the ideal place to site a new lifeboat station. In reality it was a different matter because Minehead is the point where the effects of the channel's tidal range - the world's second highest - are starkly revealed.

While high tides lap - and occasionally overtop - sea defences low spring tides can see the sea retreating well over half a mile, with the bay drying out completely.

West of the station waves break at high tide either onto remote pebble or boulder beaches or at the very foot of the soaring cliffs. There is no sand beach closer than Combe Martin, 30 miles away.

Meanwhile directly in front of the boathouse a steep pebble ridge provides one of the most difficult of launching sites: in bad weather the profile and consistency of the ridge can be altered in a single tide, making launching and recovering a lifeboat a perpetual challenge.

Once the sea retreats from the foot of the ridge areas of sand and treacherous clay are revealed, adding to the hazards to be negotiated, while on the very lowest tides the lifeboat has to be towed almost a quarter of a mile along the sands west of the station to reach water deep enough to launch into. Little wonder, then, that a number of launch vehicles have become bogged down and covered by the sea over the years.

The only advantage offered by the local topography is the fact that the mass of North Hill, rising for nearly 200 meters immediately behind the station, provides complete shelter from southerly, south-south westerly and south-south easterly winds.

On top of the hill a full gale may be blowing but in front of the station and for three miles west to Hurlestone Point the sea will be relatively calm.

Initially the George Leicester was simply sent sliding down the ridge into the sea over a bed of wooden skids (as long as the tide was in), though within two years a launch carriage was provided to make the operation slightly less hit-and-miss and enable her to launch when the tide was lower.

She was a rudimentary vessel, powered by 12 oars with an auxiliary sail. But there was no shortage of volunteers to crew her, most drawn from the families who lived in Quay Street and who at the time were involved in the local fishing industry - surnames such as James, Bushen, Martin, Webber, Slade and Escott featured prominently on the list. William Martin was the first coxswain and was to remain so for 30 years.

The George Leicester's first service, to escort a local fishing boat home in bad weather, was in December 1902. She went on to save 23 lives during 11 effective services including that in December 1910 when she saved the seven crew of the Bridgwater fishing smack M and E. But that rescue was achieved at a tragic cost: crew member William Slade suffered severe exposure during the mission, never recovered, and died - probably from pneumonia - the following year.

A routine inspection in 1927, however, revealed the George Leicester was no longer fit for service so she was replaced with the Hopwood, another 35-ft, 12-oared Liverpool class which launched twice and saved seven lives during her time at Minehead. Her years at the station had to be curtailed after she was damaged during the second of those launches and her place was taken by the Arthur Lionel, which remained on station - without once being called out - until 1939.

THERE FOR THOSE IN PERIL

Three months before the outbreak of World War Two the Kate Greatorex, Minehead's first motor lifeboat, arrived as a replacement, one of just nine 32-ft Surf type lifeboats to be built and the only one fitted with a Gill Jet propulsion system, which gave her a top speed of 6.5 knots.

She completed 20 services in 12 years but her time at Minehead was marked by another tragedy.

In December 1941 the lifeboat was called to investigate reported wreckage in Blue Anchor Bay, but coxswain John Slade decided to put out in his own fishing boat, the Mouette ('seagull' in French) and took the shore signalman Tom Escott with him.

They spotted an object in the water soon after rounding Warren Point but as they closed in on it watchers on the shore saw them and their boat disappear in a massive cloud of flame, smoke and spray. They had been killed by a German anti-ship mine. A few shattered fragments of John Slade's boat were all that remained floating when rescuers reached the scene.

Through the middle years of last RNLI naval architects worked ceaselessly to improve and refine lifeboat design and the town's last motor life boat, the Liverpool class BHMH - named for the initials of the surnames of the four donors - was considered a true state-of-the-art craft when she was displayed at the Festival of Britain prior to arriving at the station.

The BHMH had a slightly better top speed - 7.5 knots - and completed 46 services during her 22-year tour of duty. But only the skill of coxswain Stan Rawle saved her from serious damage in February 1970 as a huge wave swept her from her carriage as she was being launched into a 60mph south-westerly gale to go to the aid of a replica sailing vessel off the South Wales coast.

Rough weather launch for the George Leicester

George Leicester's first launch 1901. Wooden skids in position on beach

THERE FOR THOSE IN PERIL

Shore crew about to recover the George Leicester

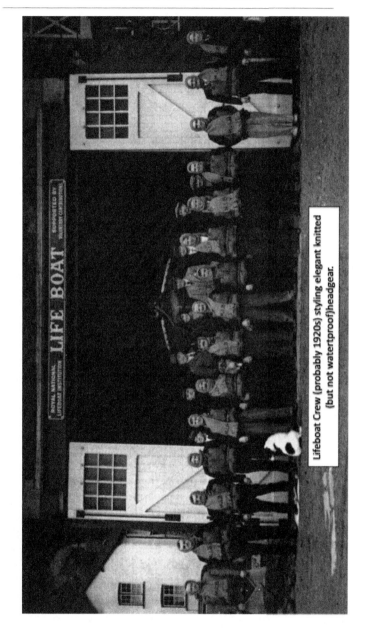

Lifeboat Crew (probably 1920s) styling elegant knitted (but not watertproof) headgear.

THERE FOR THOSE IN PERIL

A superb view of the Arthur Lionel being launched, watched by spectators on the pier. It was completed on 1901 – the same year as the lifeboat station opened - but was demolished in the war because it obstructed the field of fire of a coastal defence battery on the harbour. The guns were never fired in anger and although the pier's owners were compensated for its removal it was never rebuilt

William Martin, Coxswain 1901-31

Oars at the ready: the Arthur Lionel takes to the water

3 LIFEBOATS FOR THE NEW AGE

However in the early 1960s it began to dawn on RNLI officials that they needed to rethink the way they managed sea rescues generally around the coasts of the UK and Ireland.

Two factors were in play: in an increasingly affluent society people had more spare time on their hands and more money to spend on leisure pursuits - including boating.

But, equally, many were taking to the sea with little or no experience or, often, safety equipment and as a result the RNLI was dealing with an increasing volume of emergency calls: calls for which its fleet of slow, mainly wooden boats which could manage no more than eight knots was ill-suited.

What was required was a new type of rescue vessel. One that was small, rapid, robust, quick to launch and capable of manoeuvring among rocks or being beached, and which would perform well in surf and shallow water.

And the D class was the institution's answer: a 15-foot inflatable powered by a 40 hp outboard engine, launched directly and rapidly into the sea from its trolley and capable of carrying a crew of three and up to six survivors.

Its double-skinned inflatable sponsons were divided into airtight compartments so that if one was punctured the others would remain intact and the boat's performance would only be marginally compromised - though the boat's knife, with a specially-designed concave blade, reduced the risks of accidental deflation.

In fact the knife was one of the few bits of kit on a sparsely-equipped boat. There was a life ring attached to a throwing line, an anchor, a rudimentary first aid pack, a basic tool kit, two oars held in canvas rowlocks and stowed on top of the sponsons, and a thick mattress for the crew to kneel on and obtain a small degree of relief from a brutally uncomfortable ride.

The D class could be launched within a couple of minutes and its speed of around 22 knots enabled rapid intervention. The statistics soon began to show that inflatable lifeboats were the precise tool needed to deal with calls to the country's growing fleet of amateur sailors and to thousands of others walking, scrambling and climbing along cliffs, often ill-equipped and with no thought given to the volatile weather, the state of the tide, or the remoteness of the areas they were exploring.

Nowhere was this more apparent than at Minehead. The BHMH may have been exhibited as a thoroughly modern lifeboat at the Festival of Britain but by the late 1960s her agonisingly slow launch time and her eight-knot top speed meant she was no longer a suitable vessel for what had become one of the country's busiest holiday resorts.

4 ON SERVICE

Minehead's first D class arrived in February 1970. But if the RNLI was dealing with a radically changed clientele its new boats, similarly, required younger, fitter crews - and they were drawn from all walks of life, rather than from traditional seafaring families.

Even recruits with no seagoing experience were welcome, the RNLI confident - as it remains today - of being able to train them up to an acceptable level of competency in all the required disciplines, from boat handling, radio procedure and first aid to navigation and knots.

Derek Williams, who moved to Minehead to start a double-glazing company, was typical of those who found the idea of crewing a fast boat while helping to save lives at sea an attractive proposition - even though his only qualification was living close to the station.

"We had bought a house in Quay Street and were doing it up every week-end. After one work session I went into the pub next door and there were a couple of blokes from the crew there," he said.

"I knew one of them and he asked whether I would be interested and suggested I came down for the next Sunday morning exercise.

"I went down for two Sundays and absolutely loved it - and that was it. It was brilliant."

After being accepted as crew Derek moved up to helm and upon (compulsory) retirement became a tractor driver and then a deputy launching authority, finally retiring in 2021.

"You never ever thought about being paid for being on the crew," he said. "That thought never entered my head. We were just doing something for the community - and that was enough of a reward.

"So was the social life we had. There was an amazing camaraderie; we used to go off and visit other crews; and we had some brilliant family events all through the year."

The same story could be told by any of the volunteers who have crewed Minehead's inshore boats over the years and who have included postmen, an accountant, doctors, a tea merchant, painters, an optician, a locksmith and police officers.

The contrast with the old, conventional lifeboat could hardly have been greater. This was particularly true in terms of speed - though the far livelier pace of the D class brought with it challenges for those crewing it.

"The first time I went out smashed my face against the samson post and came back with a mouth full of blood," recalls Barry Cockrem. "But that didn't put me off: I loved it."

Barry had already been a member of the station's shore crew for some years and as soon as the BHMH was withdrawn transferred to the D class. And soon came to realise that it was capable of operating in conditions far more challenging than its relatively diminutive size might have suggested.

"You soon got to understand that the boat was better than you were," he said. "The D class could cope with far more than we had initially thought.

 "But the engine wasn't all that reliable, we only carried a hand-held torch and the tool kit would go rusty within a week. We weren't issued with any gloves and if you were practicing beach landings you got soaked - I remember going out through some surf once and so much spray was coming in the boat I couldn't breathe.

"It was only after we had been to the Boat Show and talked to one of the exhibitors that we got hold of some wet suit boots and then we bought wet suit kits and made our own."

The early D class boats lacked so much of the equipment routinely carried today that there wasn't even a radio, so communication with coastguards or rescue helicopters was impossible once the crew was at sea.

And such deficiencies often meant the crew had to be extra-resourceful. When, for instance, in July 1972 the boat was called to a climber stuck 50 feet up a cliff face at Culvercliff, west of the station, crew member David James cut off the anchor rope, scrambled up to the casualty and used it to lower him to the beach - a rescue which won him an official commendation.

Compared to today's kit, however, the crew's protection from the elements was truly basic. Modern inshore boat crews wear thermal suits inside dry suits fitted with neck and wrist seals and integral boots. In the 1970s the crews wore oilskins suits over their ordinary clothing, invariably arriving back from a job not just cold but soaked to the skin.

But the contrast with today's lifeboat service - where it takes months of training to become seagoing crew - could hardly have been starker. The volunteers who had shown an interest in crewing the new Minehead D class were given a week's intensive instruction by the RNLI's divisional inspector in early February. Then they were told to take the boat out as often as possible for the rest of the month - and to be ready to go on service from the beginning of March.

For the first couple of years Minehead was a summer-only inshore boat station but in 1973 two D class boats took over year-round duties as the Liverpool class was finally withdrawn.

That departure drew a line under an uneasy situation which had existed because of the old crew's understandable resentment at losing their boat. Relations between the two factions were always strained, often hostile, with accusations frequently levelled that neither the new crew nor their 'rubber boat' were up to the job.

Indeed the station's new boats hardly looked impressive, dwarfed as they were by the huge boat hall once occupied by the BHMH, and in the early days there was a distinct feeling the RNLI in Minehead had lost some prestige - visitors would look inside the station and remark : "Oh, they haven't got a real lifeboat, then" and walk away.

But Commander George Cooper, the RNLI's divisional inspector, lifted spirits when he declared the Minehead lifeboat station had an exciting future ahead of it. He wasn't wrong.

BHMH at sea. Coxswain Harold Bushen at the helm and his successor, Stan Rawle, standing forward of the cuddy.

THERE FOR THOSE IN PERIL

The BHMH with coxswain Joe Parsons at the wheel

THERE FOR THOSE IN PERIL

Reserve lifeboat Sarah Ann Austin being launched. Note the gasholder associated with the old Quay West gasworks and which was removed on the 1970s.

THERE FOR THOSE IN PERIL

Lifeboat Day August 1935

THERE FOR THOSE IN PERIL

The Kate Greatorex
Minehead Lifeboat 1939-1951

THERE FOR THOSE IN PERIL

Launching the Kate Greatorex

Joe Parsons, station mechanic and coxswain April-May 1973, left, and Harold Bushen, coxswain 1957-66

Coxswain John Slade aboard his ill-fated fishing boat

THERE FOR THOSE IN PERIL

Over the stones: launching the BHMH

The BHMH launching on exercise 1960

The BHMH moored in Minehead Harbour

THERE FOR THOSE IN PERIL

Recovering the BHMH

The BHMH up close

THERE FOR THOSE IN PERIL

Launching the BHMH with the Case tractor

THERE FOR THOSE IN PERIL

Night launch for the BHMH: the crew are just about to knock the retaining shackles away

The last launch of the BMH in 1973

THERE FOR THOSE IN PERIL

Last launch: the BHMH leaves the station in 1973

THERE FOR THOSE IN PERIL

Same old problem: tractor driver John Newton battles the beach to recover the Atlantic 21

THERE FOR THOSE IN PERIL

Winching from D 500. If an inshore lifeboat remains stationary it will be blown around by the downdraught so the operation has to be carried out at half speed with the helm keeping station precisely beneath the aircraft's door.

THERE FOR THOSE IN PERIL

Lifeboat day winching demonstration with the BHMH and a Westland Wessex SAR helicopter

5 BIGGER AND FASTER

Following the successful introduction of the D class the RNLI had been working on enhanced designs for more sophisticated inshore boats.

One was a stretched D class, 19ft long, carriage-launched, with two outboards and a three-man crew. A prototype sent to Minehead was found to provide a stable working platform at sea- fortunately enough, because it was non-self-righting. But it was regarded as underpowered, particularly when the crew had filled the ballast tanks it needed to cope with the short, steep seas of the Bristol Channel.

A real test of its capabilities came in September 1975 when it was launched at night into a force eight north-easterly gale to go to the aid of a 37ft yacht drifting off Hurlestone Point. Conditions were atrocious: Hurlestone Point can normally be reached from Minehead in ten minutes but on this service in a rough and confused sea and with the wind strength increasing it took an hour and a quarter.

The yacht was finally located and after several attempts at going alongside the three crew were eventually taken off and brought ashore. The service saw helm Chris Rundle and crew Albert Hartgen and Peter McGregor presented with RNLI bravery awards - the institution's thanks on vellum for Chris and vellum service certificates for the two crew.

But in a separate design stream the RNLI had also introduced rigid inflatables: fibreglass hulls topped by inflatable sponsons and with solid decks. The first was the Atlantic 21 - it was 21ft long and so named because it had been developed with the aid of students at Atlantic College on the South Wales coast. There the sixth-formers had their own lifeboat crew and there in 1969 Elizabeth Hostvedt, an 18-year-old Norwegian student, had become the first woman qualified to command an RNLI inshore lifeboat.

The Atlantic 21 was fast, manoeuvrable and a wonderful seakeeping boat. It carried three crew and was equipped for day and night work, but the RNLI was reluctant to station one at Minehead: there were fears the hull would be damaged if the craft needed to be beached anywhere to the west of the station.

An improved version of the stretched D class was sent instead but was almost immediately found unsuitable for Bristol Channel conditions - she was prone to be caught by the wind while cresting a wave and pivot alarmingly on her sponson ends, to the great concern of the crew.

Finally in 1976 the RNLI relented and Minehead's first Atlantic 21, Catherine Plumbley, arrived to take up station. Like its successors, the Atlantic 75 and 85, in the event of capsize it could be righted in around 10 seconds by activating an airbag carried on the gantry aft.

With the arrival of the Atlantic class boat the exciting times predicted by George Cooper soon materialised. The high-speed vessel was sent on missions taking her as far from station as Combe Martin, Burnham-on-sea and Steep Holm while frequently working in harness with the D class to extricate trapped walkers from the foot of the towering cliffs westward.

THERE FOR THOSE IN PERIL

Launches were counted in the dozens every year. Few were weather-related but many - entirely in line with the trend the RNLI had identified - involved calls to amateur sailors who found themselves in difficulties as a result of their inexperience, poor knowledge, or lack of equipment.

Sometimes these deficiencies had amusing outcomes such as the time when the crew, out on exercise one Sunday, encountered four men in a cabin cruiser heading merrily along the coast towards Minehead.

They waved the lifeboat alongside and asked how far it was to Newport. When Newport, Gwent, was indicated as being off to the north-east across the channel they looked puzzled and said they were actually heading for Newport, Pembrokeshire. They refused to believe that was some 35 miles away to the northwest and insisted they were navigating westwards along the coast of South Wales.

In the event it all became clear. They had bought the boat the previous day in Ilfracombe and, despite having neither compass nor lifejackets, had decided to take it home to Newport, Pembrokeshire, overnight.

Local fishermen had tried to dissuade them but they insisted on going. So they had been advised to head for Lundy Island some 12 miles offshore, motor up the western side and then remain on the same bearing until they reached the Welsh coast, at which point they should turn left.

But darkness had fallen by the time they reached Lundy and in the gloom they motored up the west coast, rounded the northern point, steamed back down the east coast and then headed for the lights of what they thought was Wales but was actually North Devon - again. Which is how, after turning left, they found themselves off Minehead and perilously low on fuel.

But lack of expertise and knowledge also resulted in tragedies, including that involving two holidaying brothers who had put out from Bossington beach in their tiny dinghy for a night's fishing. The following morning when they were reported missing Minehead's Atlantic launched and a mile or so west of Porlock Weir came across the dinghy, upside down but still at anchor. Of the brothers there was no sign.

The most likely explanation for what had happened was that the pair had failed to pay out enough anchor line and when the tide rose their dinghy had suddenly become swamped. It would have all happened in a few seconds, leaving the brothers immediately struggling in cold water.

6 GOING OUT WITH A BANG

Calls for lifeboat assistance can come at any time, as the Minehead crew has discovered.

In May 1986 they were alerted just as they were about to go into bat in a friendly cricket match against local bank staff. Sufficient crew to man the boat raced to the boathouse, launched, towed in a broken-down yacht from the middle of Porlock Bay and returned to the cricket ground in time to compete the innings - and win.

The following year a call came in the middle of the annual lifeboat service when the minister had to be abruptly bundled off the Atlantic he was using as a pulpit and yards of bunting ripped down before the boat could launch. And on another occasion came a call in late afternoon on Christmas Day, with the boat tasked to evacuate a member of the crew of a Greek coaster who had been stricken with appendicitis.

Not all casualties are human: dogs have featured prominently in the Minehead station's service list. While the RNLI may not be an official animal rescue service the policy is to rescue dogs where possible to prevent their owners attempting to do so and possibly ending up in trouble themselves.

One of the most remarkable canine rescues involved a springer spaniel called Sprig. In 2014 he was spotted by the crew of the Atlantic during their Sunday morning exercise, stranded on a rocky ledge at the foot of cliffs near Foreland Point. Because of the difficult access the D class was called in and Sprig was eventually extracted and returned to Minehead.

It was only then that the full story emerged: he had gone missing during a cliff-top walk a week earlier. Despite his owners Mark and Susie Sanders searching the cliffs and even hiring a boat to check the shoreline there had been no sign of him.

Mrs Sanders said: "We were coming to the conclusion that he must have wandered off and then been stolen.

"I just could not believe it when we had a call to say the lifeboat crew had spotted him and rescued him. It was amazing: the best news ever. Bless them."

Until a few years ago anyone living near a lifeboat station would have been aware when the boat was being launched thanks to the thunderous racket of maroons - the explosive mortar shells traditionally used as an assembly signal for lifeboat crews.

The sound of a maroon always added a note of drama to any lifeboat launch - particularly if windows were set rattling when one was fired in the quiet of the night.

Maroons were audible - in the right circumstances - up to a mile away but had to be handled with extreme caution. The shell would be lowered into a mortar set well into the ground and an eight-second timer fuse attached to allow the firer to get well clear before the first charge sent the projectile spinning nearly 200 feet into the air where it would disintegrate with an ear-shattering bang.

Mortar-fired maroons were replaced by a hand-held version: a tube just over a foot long identical to those used for firing distress and parachute flares and whose charge would be sent 350 feet in the air in a trail of smoke before exploding.

But the system was by no means perfect. The wind could muffle the sound of the maroon so some crew members failed to hear it. And the call-out procedure was still dogged by delays: after being contacted by the coastguard the operations manager still had to get to the station where the maroons were safely stored in a magazine before the crew could be alerted.

These delays contrasted oddly with the actual speed of launching. The Minehead crew have always reckoned to be at sea within seven or eight minutes of being called. And after a couple of worryingly delayed launches the decision was taken to look for a better system.

Accordingly a campaign was launched to equip the crew with pagers. The Minehead community responded with its usual generosity to a fund-raising appeal and enough money was donated to acquire the pagers and a dedicated transmitter which was housed in a redundant television relay station on the summit of North Hill.

The call-out system was incredibly efficient. By dialling one phone number the coastguard could page the operations manager and his deputy launching authorities and after being informed of the emergency they needed simply to dial another number to activate the crew pagers.

Minehead thus became one of the first stations in the country to adopt pagers - some years before the RNLI introduced them as standard for all its crews.

Maroons were still fired as a back-up, however, though Minehead came to play a significant role in their subsequent withdrawal from general use.

When lifeboats are being launched 9,000 times a year things are bound to go wrong occasionally. As they did one day at Minehead in the late 1980s when a hand-held maroon was fired. Although discharged with the usual safety precautions - aimed slightly out to sea - the missile had other ideas and a second or so after firing abruptly changed direction and in a thousand-to-one chance shot straight through the open window of the crew room, then situated up under the eaves at the front of the building.

The three crew who were getting changed into their kit were literally caught with their trousers down as the projectile expended its energy ricocheting off ceiling, walls and floor before finally exploding.

Luckily temporary deafness and a couple of light flesh wounds were the only injuries it inflicted. But the incident, together with other misfires recorded elsewhere in the country, led to the devices being withdrawn from use and hastened the general introduction of pagers.

Not that this had been the only mishap involving lifeboat pyrotechnics at Minehead. Shortly before the withdrawal of the BHMH coxswain Stan Rawle decided to celebrate the departure of the season's last pleasure steamer from the harbour by firing some time-expired parachute flares, normally used for night-time searching.

But these are wind-seeking and there was a stiff north-easterly breeze blowing. The first flare ignited and immediately drifted back over the harbour and into the vegetation on the steep slope of North Hill where it started a blaze which firemen took until the following morning to put out.

Prototype lifeboat D500 being prepared for launch

Standing room only: the D 500's helm steered from a tubular steel cockpit

THERE FOR THOSE IN PERIL

Minehead's first Atlantic 21, The Catherine Plumbley

THERE FOR THOSE IN PERIL

Atlantic 21 and D class at sea

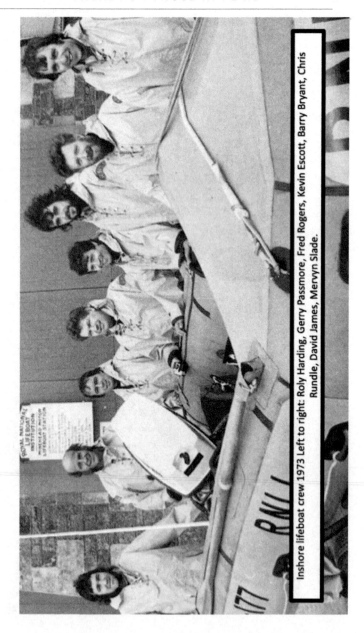

Inshore lifeboat crew 1973 Left to right: Roly Harding, Gerry Passmore, Fred Rogers, Kevin Escott, Barry Bryant, Chris Rundle, David James, Mervyn Slade.

Minehead D class crew 1976. Crew from left: Barry Bryant, Roly Harding, David James, Mike Hopper, John Newton, Terry Arnold

THERE FOR THOSE IN PERIL

Launching Minehead's first D class

Misty return: the Richard and Elizabeth Deaves returns from a Sunday launch.

7 LADIES WHO LAUNCH

If, as they say, there is no 'I' in 'team' then lifeboating represents the pinnacle of teamwork.

The normal social hierarchy is left at the boathouse door and swapped for one where experience and knowledge take precedence over everything and where a crew made up of professionals such as doctors or accountants may find themselves taking orders from the postman or plumber who's on the helm.

Those who volunteer for lifeboat duties need to be fit, reasonably good swimmers - and with sufficient time to devote to them. They absolutely must be available for training - the all-important sessions either afloat or ashore which ensure every launch to an emergency runs like clockwork. But they also need to fit in and work as a member of a dedicated and highly competent team.

Would-be recruits start as shore crew helping to launch and recover the boats before a sample trip afloat will help them decide whether they are ready to step up for training as boat crew.

Going out in a fast and pretty uncomfortable lifeboat when it's cold and wet and the sea is kicking up is not for everyone. But even membership of the shore crew still offers plenty of opportunities to play a worthwhile role in the life and work of the station.

Whether ashore or afloat there is a significant time commitment to make. The crew launch on exercise six times a month - twice at night - as well as undergoing shore-based training, attending courses and responding to an average of around 40 shouts a year.

But, says Derek Williams, everyone who volunteers needs to be able to fit in to a pretty tightly-knit community.

"It's no good people turning up behaving as they know everything, because they don't," he said.

"There is a massive amount to learn and virtually everyone who signs up has to start from scratch. And if they start acting as though they know it all and perhaps start wearing their lifeboat Guernsey to the pub just to try to impress people then they will almost certainly be asked to leave."

Traditionally lifeboat crews were all-male affairs - although many stations, particularly in East Anglia, relied on the crew's wives to haul the boat into the shallows to launch.

But the arrival of inshore boats provided a real opportunity for women to join up, even take command of a boat, as Elizabeth Hostvedt had done in 1969.

Even so it wasn't until 2008 that Minehead's first female recruit arrived. She was Karla Thresher, who was keen to uphold the family lifeboating tradition - her great-uncle, Harold Bushen, had been Minehead coxswain from 1957-66.

Karla spent her first few years as shore crew, always with an eye towards eventually joining the boat crew and going afloat. But in 2012 locksmith Raji Webber and optometrist Philippa Hales also signed up for the crew after responding to a recruitment drive organised when the station's crew list had dropped to a worryingly low number.

"One of the very first things they do is to take you out in the boat for a familiarisation trip – to show you what it can do and the sort of conditions you are likely to encounter," Raji said at the time.

"It's a make-or-break thing. A lot of people decide there and then that lifeboating is not for them and either join the shore crew or walk away completely. Others find it an exhilarating experience and immediately sign up to start training. I was one of those – and I haven't looked back.

"The RNLI is a wonderful organisation and Minehead is a wonderful station because everyone's a volunteer and we're all there for the same reason – to save lives at sea.

"When I was recruited I was informed by a couple of the crew that it was the best club in town. They weren't wrong."

Philippa meanwhile had thought about joining the crew when she moved to Minehead in 2012 - and regarded doing so as a challenge.

"It was also a chance to give something back to the community, but what I hadn't realised was that there is an awful lot to learn. And the thing that really surprised me was how supportive the crew were.

"It was a bit of a step into the unknown going out in a boat with a load of blokes but as soon as I went the first time it was great: everyone got on with teaching me all the things I needed to know."

Few people were more delighted with the arrival of women crew members than the then branch chairman, Dr Bryan Stoner, himself a former crew member. He was a great advocate for sexual equality and had long held the view that women were every bit as capable as men of crewing lifeboats and saving lives.

He regarded their arrival as a really positive step for the station.

"The place had become something of a grumpy old men's club but the women completely altered the dynamic," he said at the time.

"To the men's credit they were immediately accepted, made to feel welcome, and supported - and from that point the entire atmosphere at the station changed for the better. People were more cheerful and it felt generally like a more pleasant place to be."

By 2020 Minehead had acquired five women crew members - among the highest proportion of any station. And it could lay claim to a further distinction. Thanks to Karla being passed as D class helm - making her the first woman to command a Minehead lifeboat - the station was now one of the very few in the country capable of putting an all-woman crew to sea.

After that, indeed, there was no holding Karla back. Within a matter of months she had also become an Atlantic helm. Then in 2022 she landed a full-time RNLI job as Thames commander based at Gravesend - one of the four lifeboat stations the RNLI maintains on the Thames as far upstream as Teddington - while remaining a volunteer at Minehead between her four-day duty tours.

"It's a fantastic job," she said. "I get to go out on a lifeboat every day - and I have turned a hobby and a passion into a career."

Dr John Higgie, lifeboat operations manager at Minehead, said the fact the station had been able to provide someone to occupy such a high-profile posting was a real feather in the station's cap.

"It says a lot about the RNLI that people like Karla, who join with little or no seagoing experience, can be trained up to professional standards - and equally her appointment says a lot about the general level of ability of the Minehead crew," he said.

But if women have been enthusiastically accepted into the Minehead crew the practicalities of a having a mixed-sex team have been challenging. As a result of alterations carried out into the 1990s when the station was earmarked for an all-weather boat (the idea was eventually dropped) the only place the crew had to get changed into their kit was an open balcony.

And the only place where the women's modesty could be protected was a cramped store cupboard in the eaves - which became their domain until proper changing rooms were provided as part of the station's £1 million refurbishment in 2023.

THERE FOR THOSE IN PERIL

Ladies who launch 2018. Left to right: Raji, Tracy, Karla, Philippa, Meghan

THERE FOR THOSE IN PERIL

Sunday morning Lifeboat veterans club (from left) David James, Barry Cockrem, Derek Williams, Barry Bryant.

THERE FOR THOSE IN PERIL

Atlantic 85 returning after unsuccessful search for a pot of gold

THERE FOR THOSE IN PERIL

Launching the Atlantic 85 with the RNLI designed Talus unit

THERE FOR THOSE IN PERIL

The Talus tractor is older than many of the crew!

THERE FOR THOSE IN PERIL

Atlantic 85 Richard and Elizabeth Deaves at sea

Richard and Elizabeth Deaves being recovered after exercise

The Atlantic 85 off to do service

THERE FOR THOSE IN PERIL

The Lifeboat station 2024 "One Crew"

THERE FOR THOSE IN PERIL

Launching the station's latest Atlantic 85 Penny J II

One of the RNLI's articulated, tracked launch vehicles - known as a bendy - undergoing trials in 2023 to assess its suitability for launching Minehead's Atlantic 85. The trials were unsuccessful.

THERE FOR THOSE IN PERIL

Just how tricky launching conditions can be: in 2013 Minehead's Case launching tractor became bogged down in deep clay during a low water launch - and so did a Talus tractor sent to recover it.

THERE FOR THOSE IN PERIL

Both vehicles were covered by the tide and recovered the following day, the waterproofed Talus still in full working order, the Case, alas, not

8 FIT FOR THE FUTURE

If there was ever any doubt about the wisdom of stationing inshore lifeboats at Minehead it would have been comprehensively swept away by the station's 2022 statistics: 40 launches, 10 lives saved - and dozens more casualties rescued.

But those figures should be looked at in more detail. Generally RNLI lifeboats launch around 9,000 times a year and help thousands of people. But every launch is carefully assessed and only a small fraction end up being classified as 'life saved' - in other words but for the intervention of a lifeboat crew someone would have died.

In 2022 there were 9,312 lifeboat launches and 389 lives saved - so Minehead's contribution was significant. But five of those 10 lives saved related to a single incident. More remarkably still it took place only yards from the boathouse - but still offered evidence of how the Bristol Channel can be a dangerous place.

The five were holidaymakers who had hired paddle boards. It was the first time any of them had tried the sport and they found the challenge of returning to shore against a falling tide and an offshore wind too much. Eventually they became so exhausted they were unable to climb back onto their boards when they fell off. All five were pulled from the water just 50 yards outside the harbour.

For the rest of 2022 the calls followed the usual annual pattern: walkers missing or trapped under the cliffs, exhausted swimmers and occasional mishaps, such as vessels breaking down or anglers aboard charter boats injuring themselves.

But the overwhelming majority of launches continue to be to people either unaware of or underequipped for conditions in the Bristol Channel.

Its huge tidal range of up to 14 metres means the currents flow far more quickly than someone can either swim, or paddle a kayak - and trying to do either against the tide can quickly lead to exhaustion.

And even with radar and other navigational aids locating casualties is never easy, particularly in the dark, because currents can quickly carry them away from their last reported position.

Such was the case in 2019 when the Atlantic was launched to look for two kayakers who had failed to return after setting out from Porlock Weir with the aim of paddling to Hurlestone Point. As they headed back they had found the tide running too fast to make any headway against. As it got dark a third kayaker had managed to struggle ashore and raised the alarm.

But although the lifeboat made all speed to the scene and began searching nothing could be found. And kayaks are so low in the water they will not show up on a radar screen. Eventually a coastguard helicopter equipped with a thermal imaging camera located the pair - well over a mile away from their last reported position.

The calls have settled into a regular pattern. There are the occasional mishaps, such as vessels breaking down or anglers aboard charter boats injuring themselves, but the overwhelming majority of launches are to people either unaware of or underequipped for conditions in the Bristol Channel.

Its huge tidal range of up to 14 metres means the currents flow far more quickly than someone can either swim, or paddle a kayak - and trying to do either against the tide can quickly lead to exhaustion.

Minehead is also the starting point for the South West Coast Path which runs for 630 miles round Land's End and along the south coast to Poole. Nine million walkers use it every year but a number of those setting out from Minehead either ignore or miss the direction signs and attempt to make their way along the beach to Hurlestone Point, only to find themselves trapped by the incoming tide.

Most, luckily, carry mobile phones and can call for help - and advising them merely to wait for the tide to go down is never an option. If a casualty is trapped in the afternoon or on a summer evening it will probably be dark before the sea retreats and only the best-equipped will be able to self-rescue at that point. The alternative is a long, cold and uncomfortable night while the tide comes in again, and only retreats once daylight has returned.

And even the most experienced walkers can be beaten by the local conditions: in 2021 a Coventry woman set out from Minehead to walk round the entire coast of the UK. She had covered just three miles before becoming cut off by the tide and having to be rescued.

But whatever the emergency the RNLI's Minehead station is now better equipped than ever to deal with it thanks to a £1 million-plus, year-long project which has seen it enlarged and modernised.

The original station had already been extended in the 1990s: seamlessly, with the front of the building being dismantled stone by stone and moved 19 feet forward with the gap filled by local sandstone matching the original.

But it was remodelled internally for an all-weather boat - and not for the needs of inshore lifeboat crews who often arrive back from a shout very cold and very wet after hours at sea in an open boat. The station had no changing rooms and only one rudimentary shower. The crew room was too small to accommodate all the crew for meetings or, particularly, training sessions. And valuable minutes were lost every time the D class launched because its tractor was housed in a separate garage at the rear of the building.

All that has now changed. Land was bought next to the station to allow it to be extended with the creation of a spacious crew room and galley on the first floor, changing rooms and showers on the ground floor and a separate boat hall where, permanently hitched to its launch vehicle, is the D class, the Exmoor Belle, much of the cost of which was donated locally and which was so named - after a competition held at her school - by Lilia Guscott, whose grandfather, Steve, served on the Minehead crew for several years.

.

9 FIT FOR PURPOSE

As the first inshore lifeboat crews quickly discovered, spending more than a few minutes aboard a fast, open boat with no shelter from the elements can be a highly uncomfortable experience.

Equally it has always been recognised that lifeboat crew members who are cold and wet will be unable to work efficiently and may well imperil the rest of the crew, their boat - or, most importantly, the casualty.

Which is why the RNLI has devoted so much energy and ingenuity to developing protective clothing specific to inshore boat crews. The simple, all-purpose oilskin suits which were the initial issue have long since gone. They were replaced by wetsuits for a time before designers came up with the ultimate product: an all-in-one dry suit with integral boots, watertight seals at the wrist and neck and a waterproof zip.

These are worn on top of a onesie-style 'woolly-bear' suit over their normal clothes.

Going equipped: helm Richard Gay modelling what a well-dressed crew member will wear.

Minehead Lifeboat station before the rebuild.

And after......

Minehead's D Class: D847 Exmoor Belle

THERE FOR THOSE IN PERIL

B-824 Richard & Elizabeth Deaves, Mineheads B class for 16 years

Minehead's Atlantic 85 Penny J II heads out after her official naming in October 2023

And they are compulsory wear on each and every shout. A lifeboat may be called out on a balmy summer day for what appears to be a straightforward, there-and-back rescue. But no-one can tell how long it will be at sea. What appears to be a simple operation may well turn into a protracted search, or another emergency may arise when the boat's out. And without the proper clothing the wind chill factor can be debilitating.

On top of the dry suit is worn - at all times - the all-important lifejacket; another essential item whose design the RNLI has constantly improved and refined over the years. From the very start inshore lifeboat crews were provided with jackets which would keep them floating face up, even when unconscious, but the current issue is the most sophisticated design yet.

It comes equipped with a red smoke flare, a satellite GPS personal locator beacon, a whistle, torch and knife along with a safety line to attach to a boat.

Only in the very early days did the RNLI look to off-the-shelf commercial craft for its inshore fleet. Nowadays all inshore boats are built in-house at the inshore lifeboat base in East Cowes, a centre of excellence in the design and construction of inflatable craft which has won it an international reputation - and orders from other lifeboat services, including Holland's.

Building on nearly 60 years of experience and feedback from its crews the RNLI has ceaselessly added innovations and refinements to create rescue craft which are among the world's most sophisticated.

Crew comfort has been improved, equipment upgraded and safety features enhanced with the Atlantic 85 and its suite of sophisticated navigation instrumentation representing the pinnacle of inshore lifeboat development.

In parallel with upgrading its boats the RNLI has had to call on its reserves of ingenuity to improve its launch vehicles, designed in-house and built mainly by Powys-based specialists Clayton Engineering.

The Minehead inshore crew originally inherited the station's Case tractor, a tracked vehicle which could be driven into the sea to launch either boat though could not - as a number of unscheduled experiments revealed - survive being completely submerged.

The Case was simple to drive: two sets of levers offered high and low range drive and forward and reverse gearing for each track, making it highly manoeuvrable. But on numerous occasions beach conditions proved too much for it and it had to be pulled up using the massive winch which stood at the rear of the boat hall until the 1990s remodelling.

A succession of various Case models were succeeded by the Talus, an RNLI-designed, nine-litre engine tractor originally designed to launch all-weather boats but, currently, the only fleet vehicle capable of coping with Minehead's challenging launch location - where the incline even requires the cradle on the Atlantic 85 launch carriage to be remotely raised to keep the boat more or less level as it approaches the water.

In the event of bogging down the Talus's waterproof hatches mean it can survive submersion unharmed.

Meanwhile the station's D class is pushed into the sea by a Tooltrak, a specifically designed, compact rubber-tracked vehicle easily steered by joystick. The station was among the first to be issued with one.

Though, as was discovered in January 2018, it is not a vehicle which takes kindly to being submerged under several feet of sea water.

The crew were called when a woman who was trying to make her way across the beach to the harbour became trapped in chest-deep mud on an incoming tide. Technically this was a mud rescue job for the coastguard but although the local coastguard team were alerted they merely watched the operation from the harbour, their officer explaining that they 'had not been mud-trained'.

It was impossible for the D class to get near her but the crew took the Tooltrak as close as they could and managed to extricate the casualty - though then found they could not extricate the vehicle.

10 THE LIFEBOAT FAMILY

Lifeboating has traditionally been a family affair. Many of the current crews at the RNLI's 238 stations have followed their fathers and grandfathers into the service - and Minehead is no exception.

Deputy launching authority Andrew Escott followed his father, Kevin, onto the crew at the station where his grandfather Charlie had served as winchman in the days of the wooden boats. Casualties are today as likely to be rescued by a boat commanded by Phil Sanderson as by one with his son, Jake, at the helm.

And RNLI branch chairman Richard Newton has re-joined the crew he originally became part of in his teens, inspired by his father, John - then the station tractor driver.

"I really got the bug from a very young age because of Dad's involvement," he said. "As soon as I was old enough I joined up but then work took me away and I didn't live near enough to the sea to keep up the connection.

"But it was always my ambition to get involved again as soon as I retired and came back to Minehead."

Most of the crew will acknowledge that they also feel part of the wider lifeboat family: a sense of belonging to a 9,000-strong community of volunteers united by a single purpose - that of saving lives at sea.

But at any lifeboat station the crew manning or launching the boat only represent the visible portion of the iceberg. Invisible but equally important is a supporting team of volunteers helping to raise funds towards the £188 million the RNLI needs to find every year to maintain its boats and crews at immediate readiness 24 hours a day.

As the need for serious fund-raising has increased so has the effort devoted to bringing in local revenue. Before the remodelling in the 1990s the Minehead station boasted nothing more than a small display case offering a tiny range of RNLI-branded souvenirs.

Now its modern, brightly-lit shop trades all summer and at week-ends right through the winter, staffed on a rota by a team of more than 50 volunteers and offering a huge range of RNLI merchandise.

General fund-raising, too, has been transformed. Once that was the province of the Ladies' Lifeboat Guild, a hangover from the very early days of the RNLI, which organised one or two events a year.

But the station now boasts a dynamic fund-raising team organising or attending fund-raising events all year round, staffing street and supermarket collections, and actively promoting the work of the RNLI in the local community.

It's a community which has always responded generously to any appeal for funds to keep the lifeboats on station. But that is perhaps true of any township where there is a lifeboat station. For those living away from the coast and who only go there for holidays the link is not so strong, the willingness to give not so deeply entrained.

Street collectors standing among crowds of holidaymakers will be ignored more often than not and generally speaking it's the over-40s or indeed over-50s who are more likely to donate to charity now as young families struggle with rising living costs.

And the move towards a nearly cashless society sparked by the pandemic has proved another obstacle: far fewer people actually carry money with them now which is why the RNLI has adopted the use of portable card machines.

Despite their operational commitments the crew have always found time to run their own fundraisers, hosting jazz nights and hog roasts in the station, annually staging - for 30 years - one of the UK's biggest raft races and signalling the start of everyone's Christmas celebrations with an evening of carols in the boathouse.

Richard Newton says that is probably the event in the calendar the crew look forward to most.

"It's a really enjoyable evening," he said. "We even have a couple of lifeboat supporters who travel down from Staffordshire every year just to attend and they always tell us they wouldn't miss it for the world.

"It is not so much a fund-raising event as such; just a way of thanking the local community for the way they support us during the year.

"Few local people are aware when we get a shout, but they do know we are there on call day and night ready to help anyone - and the way the money came rolling in for the new extension demonstrated just how generously they support us.

"Getting together with them once a year to celebrate Christmas is, I hope, a way of showing how much we appreciate and value that support."

ABOUT THE AUTHOR

Chris Rundle has had a long career in journalism and public relations. He was a member of Minehead lifeboat crew for 20 years, retiring as senior helm in 1990, and has since spent several years as the station's press officer.

Printed in Great Britain
by Amazon